*This groundbreaking book puts all the information you need to
make good decisions on child care in one place.*

— TESTIMONIALS —

"In today's world it's become more and more obvious that parents (and grandparents) need to be very cautious as to who they entrust their children to for child care. Your book brings up so many important issues for parents to consider, and even provides wonderful checklists and worksheets full of questions that should be considered, and asked of child care professionals, before hiring them. And the Resources List you provide make this an invaluable guide in helping make educated decisions in each of these matters.

I recommend your book every chance I get to parents, grandparents, day care centers, churches, and anyone concerned about the safety of our children in the care of others.

MARK HENDRICKS — AUTHOR, EDUCATOR AND COACH — TRILBY, FL

What a wonderful reference you've put together in "A Parent's Guide to Locating Responsible Child Care." How I wish I'd have had this reference when my daughters were still small! The resource section alone would have saved me hours of time and tons of frustration when I was trying to determine the best method of providing childcare for my children. Unfortunately, I would have given anything to have had the information in the "abuse" section when I was helping a friend through a very trying time some years back.

Every parent of younger children NEEDS this book!

ROD HAMMER — MUSICIAN AND BUSINESSMAN — INDIANAPOLIS, IN

What can I say —- your new book is absolutely filling a great need. It took me back several years when I just couldn't leave my first child with a babysitter or childcare until he was one year old, and that was just for a few hours. Both our families were in other states and I too was totally wrapped in fear, thinking that only I could take care of my new child, I just could not trust anyone.

My life would have been so much easier if I'd had this book to learn all the services that were available to me and all the procedures you point out that teach how to investigate each situation so the parents can have peace of mind and truly enjoy their children. Every family should have this book available in their home. You have covered all necessary situations and in great detail. Nothing is missing, Ron. I look forward to sharing this book with my own grown children so they have all this information at their fingertips.

LOUISE BARTH — JACKSONVILLE, FL

— TESTIMONIALS —

Thank you for creating "A Parent's Guide to Locating Responsible Child Care." I wish this guide had been available when my children were small, as it would have encouraged me to be more careful when choosing a day care. We had one bad experience with my son when he was a baby that we don't want anyone else to have. If this guide had been available to follow at that time, I would not have made the mistake that led to the bad experience. I am passing my copy of this on to my daughter to use when seeking a daycare provider for my grandson.

This guide is very complete and thorough. It lists the exact steps that you should take when choosing a babysitter and the various types of day care options that are open to parents. It even lists the various state agencies that have regulatory jurisdiction over day care providers. This is the most comprehensive child protection guide that I have read and would recommend it to any parent or concerned grandparent.

JERRY STEARNS — WWW.YOURLIFEAFTER50.COM — FARGO, ND

Wow! A fantastic, all-inclusive manual on keeping our children safe in the hands of others. Although my child is already in daycare, I now know that I did not evaluate it carefully. It was chosen based solely on convenience. Because of your book, I am now armed with questions that I hadn't even thought to ask. I also appreciate the parts on watching out for signs of abuse. Thank you for the great resource!

QUINTON SMITH — RICHMOND, VA

I found your book "A Parents Guide to Locating Responsible Child Care" to be both informative and to the point. Your section on "Responsibilities as an Employer" is something every parent should consider when choosing a caregiver. In today's world, it is no longer simply a matter of getting the kid next door to babysit.

Evaluating the "Educational Environment" of any caregiver is especially important. Developing social skills, learning and play should all be a part of a child's daily activities, whether at home or away. And the "Babysitter Quick Reference Kit" is undoubtedly the most most valuable information a parent can provide a caregiver.

Your book will be a valuable addition to every parent's library. I recommend this to parents and grandparents alike!

JIM BERRY — WATAUGA, TN

More Testimonials appear beginning on page 79

A Parent's Guide to Locating Responsible Child Care: Discover How to Create A Safer Environment for Your Child

DEDICATION

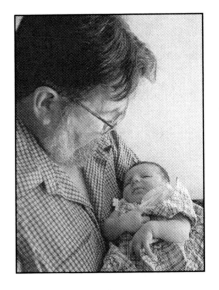

The author of this book, Dr. Ron Capps, would like to introduce the world to his youngest granddaughter Zoë Capps. Zoë was born at 9:30 pm on October 16, 2007.

During the past sixty years, the challenges confronting parents and grandparents have expanded beyond all expectations.

With increasing mobility, the contemporary American family lives a lifestyle very different from that experienced by their ancestors.

As a parent of two sons and Grandfather of three, I found it important to develop this "Parent's Guide to Locating Responsible Child Care: Discover How to Create a Safer Environment for Your Child" as a guide to share with his youngest son and his wife as they awaited the birth of their first child.

I would like to dedicate this book to my grandchildren — Zoë, Mckenzie and Johnny and to all of the parents, grandparents and others who are interested in creating a safer environment for the children of the world.

SIX THINGS THIS BOOK WILL HELP YOU ACHIEVE

1. Create a safer environment for your child.

2. Effectively screen your child care provider(s).

3. Increase your knowledge in selecting a competent child care provider.

4. Locate the absolute best child care providers in your area.

5. Decrease the chances of child care abuse.

6. Feel confident that your child is in good care when you're not present.

This book will help determine you and your child's needs, create a safer environment and help you select the absolute best child care your area has to offer without putting your child at risk.

TABLE OF CONTENTS

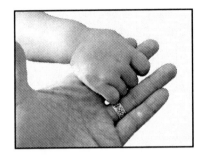

INTRODUCTION

If this book helps even one family protect their child from abuse and neglect at the hands of a caregiver, then this publication has been an overwhelming success.

Having looked everywhere for a similar guide for screening and selecting a responsible caregiver, and after not being able to find anything to help parents know how to provide their child with the best and safest care possible, I was prompted to write this book.

As you read through this book it is imperative that you understand why steps are taken, why questions are asked, and the importance of teaching your child about their safety and security.

Children need to be safe and secure and it is your responsibility as a parent and as a human being to teach them and educate them about exactly what abuse and neglect is. You must establish a relationship with your child and create a nurturing and stable environment for them to open up and talk with you.

It is also important for you to take the time to listen to them anytime they feel they want to talk, regardless of what you are doing. If you take the time and put your child before anything else you have going on in your life you will find that they will come to you whenever they have a problem, before it's too late.

You will also discover how to recognize a problem with your caregiver and what you can do about it to resolve the problem.

There is a lot of information covered in this publication with lots of tips and points to help you, as a parent, through the process of selecting top quality child care. It is recommended that you first read through this book in its entirety then go back to the detailed Table of Contents and select the specific chapters you are looking for to make your search for child care easier, quicker and safer.

You as a parent,
have the right to check
and visit any daycare,
crèche, or after-school
that you might find suitable
for your child's needs.

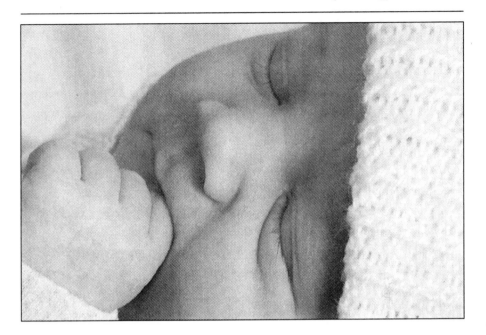

— Chapter One —
Types of Child Care

From the occasional babysitter to full-time day or after-school care, this chapter will give you specific details about the several different types of child care and what each of them can offer you and your child.

It's extremely important for you to understand the different types of child care available and what each of them can offer to your specific needs. This is the first step in your search for safe and secure child care.

Babysitters

A babysitter is someone who looks after your child occasionally. Choosing a babysitter is just as important as choosing any other type of child care.

The applicant should be carefully screened and found competent to care for your child while you're away, even for just a few hours.

It is recommended that your babysitter be older than *16 years of age because anyone who is younger cannot be charged with neglect or ill treatment of your child left in their care, if such an unfortunate incident were to happen.

If you leave your child with anyone under the age of *16 you are still responsible for them. If anything should go wrong and you are found to have left your child with someone unsuitable, which includes someone underage, you could be charged with neglect.

Nannies

Nannies are ultimately your child's nurse and daily care provider. They should have completed a course in child care, and at least one year of experience gained while studying for their qualifications.

The nannies are generally 20 years of age and up. Salaries range from $385 to $618 a week depending on experience and years of employment in other homes.

Maternity Nannies

Maternity nannies live in your home and specialize in the care of a newborn baby.

Duties would include bottle making, feeding, bathing, washing the baby's clothing, diaper changing and would be regarded as taking complete control of the newborn baby for its first few weeks at home.

Maternity nannies usually stay in the home for about four weeks but could stay up to three months, depending on the child's and or parents needs.

Salaries are at the high end of the scale, earning as much as $170 on a regular 12 hour night and increasing dramatically for multiple births and longer hours.

Mother's Helpers

Mother's helpers are ones who are wanting to start a career in the child care industry and are currently undergoing full-time, evening or home study courses.

Their experience in the child care field will have been gained within their own families, or they have been babysitting for quite some time.

* It is advisable that you check your own state laws regarding exact age.

Salaries can range between $368 to $392 per 40 hour work week, depending on their experience and your needs as a client.

Au-Pairs

Au-Pairs are, generally, foreign nationals between the ages of 18 and 26 with women over the age of 20 being mostly sought after because of their maturity level.

These foreign nationals are granted a special one year student visa, which is non-renewable.

The Au-Pair position provides a great opportunity for these young women who will frequently expect to live near a college and be able to attend English and ESL classes.

The hosting family provides room and board and a weekly stipend, and the Au-Pair will undertake light housework and child care type duties.

Presently there are eleven US government authorized agencies who arrange Au-Pair matches. The typical fee, which includes airfare, agency fees, and weekly stipend, is approximately $14,000 US per year.

Day Care (Crèche, After-School)

You as a parent, have the right to check and visit any daycare, crèche, or after-school that you might find suitable for your child's needs. You should also be aware of the things to look for when visiting these places, such as;

- Are you and your child greeted, and made to feel welcome and comfortable?
- Are the children active and do they seem to be happy?
- Are there adequate and suitable toys for the children?
- Are there adequate activities within the care center?
- Are there enough staff members present to care for the children?
- What kinds of foods are provided and are they suitable, nutritious and enough?
- What are the qualifications and experience of the staff members?
- What are the protocols of the care center for injuries?
- What are the protocols when a child becomes ill?

- Are the surroundings, both indoors and outdoors, clean and attractive?
- What are the costs of the child care center?
- Are there any programs or financial assistance available?
- Are the children ever alone with a single staff member?
- What are the protocols for resting, changing clothes, and toileting?
- Is the staff required to provide references?
- Does all the staff undergo a criminal record and background check?
- What forms of discipline are used?

Once you have a daycare in mind, call and ask them when the best time would be for you and your child to look through the facilities and learn more about what they offer.

Pre-School (Nursery School)

Pre-schools are designed to give your child an educational type program to prepare them for kindergarten and elementary school. There are also many daycare centers that incorporate early childhood curriculum in their programs.

The child will spend most of their time playing and working with materials, participating in various activities throughout the day, and interacting with other children.

The staff members or teachers will work with small groups of children as well as each one individually throughout the course of the day.

Signs of a great pre-school include:

- The classroom is decorated with various children's artwork and projects.
- The pre-school incorporates the learning of numbers and the alphabet throughout the child's daily interaction and experiences.
- The children have long periods of playing and exploring time.
- Worksheets are used rarely, if at all.
  The development of your child's creativity will be better utilized if they are able to discover their own interests as opposed to being classified, marked and graded by worksheets.

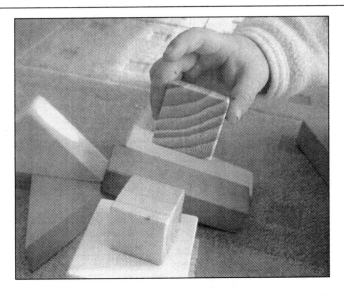

- The children have a safe outdoor play area that is used daily and is supervised.
- The teachers read books to the children individually as well as in small groups.
- The curriculum is adopted for those who are ahead as well as those who need additional help. The qualifications of the teachers will be especially important for children who are less developed in certain aspects of the curriculum.
- The children and their parents look forward to school. This is a great sign that the school is fun for your child.

In-Home Care

An in-home care provider may live in the home or outside the home but provides one-on-one contact and child care in the child's own home. The in-home care provider may also be asked to perform light household duties.

In-home care is a great alternative as opposed to trying to juggle other childcare arrangements with heavy work schedules, business trips, and overtime.

Au-pairs and nannies provide in-home care and have a typical work week of 40 to 60 hours.

Before welcoming any child care provider into your home ensure that you take the time to properly screen them before, during, and after the interview.

You must also make sure that you follow up on any information given by the applicant, especially talking with references they provide.

ADVANTAGES	DISADVANTAGES
Child stays in familiar surroundings	Child's interaction with other children is quite limited
One-to-one contact and attention with care provider	If the quality of care is poor, the child will suffer
Child doesn't have to commute with parents to and from the home	If nanny is ill or decides to leave suddenly this may cause unexpected problems
There is no pressure on the parents to send the child out of the home when the parents are ill	It can be difficult to deal with the intrusion of someone else in the home on a daily basis
Parents are not as rushed in the morning to get the child ready	Can be costly, especially if nanny is professionally qualified

Out-of-Home Care

There are several types of out-of-home child care programs available. These include *daycare centers,* which are generally affiliated with public or private agencies such as religious organizations, corporations, and community centers.

Family daycare programs, which are held in the caregiver's home. Part-time child care programs such as *pre-schools or play groups.* Publicly funded preschool programs such as *Head Start.*

All of these programs usually care for children from birth to age five. After the age of five, you will need to look into after-school care facilities in your state or province.

The American Academy of Pediatrics (AAP) recommends that one adult should have primary responsibility for no more than one baby under twelve months of age in any caregiver setting.

These younger children require positive and consistent caregiver attention who will learn to recognize the child's unique cues for hunger, distress, and play.

This kind of nurturing and interaction contributes significantly to an infant's social and emotional development. For infants, the AAP recommends a child to staff ratio of 3:1.

The differences in group size will depend on the age of your child and the number of staff the center has. Below is a table of child to staff ratios based on age, as recommended by AAP.

Age	Child to Staff Ratio	Maximum Group Size
Birth - 24 months	3:1	6
25 - 30 months	4:1	8
31 - 35 months	5:1	10
3 years	7:1	14
4 - 5 years	8:1	16

Child Care Facilities

Daycare can be provided in the caregiver's own home, often with only one single adult supervising and caring for the children. Daycare centers and pre-schools offer several adult supervisors employed by the school to care for much larger groups of children.

The American Academy of Pediatrics (AAP) **[www.aap.org]** and the National Association for the Education of Young Children (NAEYC) **[www.naeyc.org]** recommend that both types of child care facilities be licensed and regularly inspected, which you have the right to ask for when checking out their facilities.

All caregivers should have the minimum training in CPR and early childhood education and development certificates. You should also be able to find clearly written policies on forms of discipline and what the center does when a child is sick.

The center you choose will most likely be determined by the ongoing child development programs, quality of care, and well laid out policies. You may also want to look for an accreditation with the National Association for Family Child Care (NAFCC) **[www.nafcc.org/include/default.asp]**, which the center can apply for and obtain on a voluntary basis.

Child Care Center Helpful Tips

Ensure that all other children and staff members have been kept current with immunizations. You should also ask whether each staff member undergoes a criminal background check and if they are all clear.

You must also be made aware of good hygiene and safety policies which might include staff wearing disposable gloves when changing diapers, all toys are disinfected regularly, and hands are frequently washed by both staff and children to minimize the spread of germs and infections.

Another important factor you should consider is the turn-over-rate of the center's caregivers. A high rate means that their could be something wrong with the center or with how they screen their employees.

Children with Special Needs

Federal law guarantees special education and related services to children with disabilities from birth through age 5.

Special services such as speech, physical and occupational therapy can now be contracted into day care centers or preschools so that children with special needs can be included in "regular" care settings.

Early intervention services can be coordinated through your local Office of Mental Health/Mental Retardation for children up to age 3 and through your state's Department of Education for ages 3 to 5.

It is important that you take a moment now to register your copy of "A Parent's Guide to Locating Responsible Child Care." Please visit http://www.childcare-guide.info/updatedresources.html to receive access to updates, supplements and bonus gifts.

As a parent it is your responsibility to know who you are entrusting with your child. You need to know you can depend on this individual to give the best possible care to your child.

— CHAPTER TWO —

What Parents Should Know

What Makes a Good Babysitter?

A good babysitter will realize that the most important job they have is the responsibility of caring for your child.

Maturity, good judgment, and someone who likes children are the basic requirements you are looking for in a babysitter. You are also looking for someone who will entertain and do fun activities with your child.

The babysitter should also know something about child behavior, be able to handle basic needs of your child such as meals, putting the child to bed, and have the training to deal with any problems or emergencies that may arise.

Entrusting someone to care for your child can be a difficult thing to do. Finding a qualified babysitter requires time and effort, but your reward is assurance that your child is in capable hands.

The recommendations of people you know and trust are your best bet for finding a reliable and capable babysitter. If you're new to the area and don't know how to go about finding a sitter, ask your neighbors or co-workers for recommendations, or inquire at your place of worship.

Interviewing prospective sitters and checking their references will give you peace of mind. You may want to invite the sitter over for a "dry run" while you are at home so you can familiarize her with your household and observe how she interacts with your child.

Your Responsibilities as a Parent

As a parent it is your responsibility to know who you are entrusting with your child. You need to know you can depend on this individual to give the best possible care to your child. Listed below are some considerations you should keep in mind when choosing a babysitter for your child.

- Select your babysitter and also have a list of two or three other qualified babysitters in case of last minute emergencies.
- Ask your friends, relatives or neighbors if they can recommend someone they have found to be reliable.
- Get to know your babysitter before hand and have them visit your home to meet and get comfortable with your child.
- State exactly what you expect of your babysitter and make a list or emergency kit of instructions for them to follow. Discourage your babysitter from inviting and entertaining their friends in your home.
- Make it clear that the use of your telephone or their personal cell phone for personal calls is not permitted. In an emergency situation you want to be able to contact them, not get a busy signal.
- Do not accept the services of any friends of your babysitter, should they be unavailable. You cannot be sure that they will be suitable if you have not had a chance to get to know them yourself.
- Make a list of emergency numbers as well as the number you can be reached at and place by every phone in your house.
- The age of your babysitter is recommended to be at least 16 years. Depending on your state laws, it could be illegal to leave children in the care of someone under 16 years of age.
- Have a new babysitter meet you and your child in your home before their actual work night. This will give you a chance to go over

important information as well as give your babysitter a chance to meet your child.

- Provide a list of instructions about the usual bedtime routine, including the time you expect your child to be in bed, and any other information about your child they should know, such as, medicine, medical conditions etc.
- Show your babysitter around areas of the house they will need to be familiar with such as the main power shut-off switch, all exits from the home, and where they can find things such as clean clothes, diapers, and bedding.

Your Responsibilities as the Employer

When you hire a babysitter you automatically become an employer. Few parents realize this fact and even though you might not have to pay additional taxes you are still liable under the employment act.

One of the responsibilities of employing a babysitter is to inform them of all emergency contacts and procedures. This will help ensure that your babysitter is confident in knowing what to do, should an emergency arise.

- Make sure your babysitter knows when to use 9-1-1 if it applies in your area.
- Ensure that you show your babysitter where all of the doors and windows are located and how to lock/unlock them.
- Show where the first-aid supplies are kept, and ensure your babysitter knows how to use them.
- Brief your babysitter about allergies, medications or other medical information about your child.
- Indicate what TV programs, music or computer games or usage is allowed or not allowed.
- Establish rules regarding visitors, whether it be your babysitter's or your children's friends.
- If required, explain how to use certain appliances.
- Overall, ensure your babysitter understands the routines of your household. Some examples of routines you might include: bedtimes, snacks, chores, activities and homework.

- Arrange transportation to and from home for the babysitter.
- Let your babysitter know what time to expect you home, and ensure that you phone if that changes.
- Call your babysitter at least once while you are out and make sure all is well.

Employing a Babysitter

It is important that you feel confident in your babysitter's abilities and maturity level to handle any situation. You should also be aware of important information you need to give your babysitter.

- Check all references of a babysitter in exactly the same way as you would a nanny.
- Check that they know basic first aid and how to cope in an emergency.
- Tell the babysitter where you are going. If possible leave a land line contact number as well as your mobile phone number in case there is a signal problem or, if you are going to a party, it may be too loud to hear your mobile phone ringing.
- Make sure you have contact details and an address for your babysitter in case one of your children is ill or upset after you return and need to talk to her urgently.
- Don't just bolt out of the door as soon as the babysitter arrives. Make time to show her around and give any last minute instructions or details. If there are older children she needs to know what they are and aren't allowed to do with regard to television and snacks and what time they go to bed.
- Remember the babysitter doesn't know your children. If they have special words or favorite stuffed animals and blankets that get them off to sleep your babysitter needs to be told.
- Leave a contact number of someone nearby who you trust, perhaps a neighbor or relative, in case your babysitter needs on the spot help urgently.
- If your child is ill don't leave the child with a new babysitter, it isn't fair to either of them.

- Regardless of whether the parents are smokers, smoking by the babysitter should be absolutely forbidden for 3 reasons:
  — The children will be exposed to secondhand smoke.
  — There is a possibility that the children could get access to matches or a lighter.
  — It introduces a fire hazard into the home.
- Always tell your child in the morning and keep reminding them during the day that a babysitter is coming. If they don't like being left it is still much better to tell them. Sneaking off while they are playing and hoping for the best never works.
- Always overestimate rather than underestimate what time you will be home. It is better to return early than leave your babysitter hanging.
- Don't leave your child with a babysitter they don't like — take the time to find one that they get along with.

Conducting Interviews

Write down the babysitter's name, address, telephone number and drivers license number (if applicable). Ask for references such as teachers, counselors, past employers, relatives, friends, neighbors, etc.

To make this step easier you should utilize the babysitter forms that came with this publication located in the free bonuses section of this book. Get the prospective babysitter to provide all of the information which includes everything mentioned above. You will use this information to conduct a background check on their references, qualifications, honesty, reliability, etc.

Interview several prospective sitters personally and observe their interaction with your child. Interview the candidate as if they're being hired for a real job — which they are!

Interview the candidate you're considering at your house so you can see firsthand how they interact with your child.

Find out whether she's ever cared for a child the same age as your child and if you have an infant younger than 1, you want a sitter who has experience with babies. You also want to know the types of activities and games she plays with children to entertain them, and what she does when they cry or refuse to go to bed.

It's not enough that the babysitter seems responsible and likes kids. You must ensure that they also know how to keep kids from getting hurt and what to do in an emergency.

Ask a potential sitter whether she knows first aid, CPR, and the Heimlich maneuver. You can get a sense of how well she thinks on her feet by posing "What if?" scenarios, such as "What would you do if my baby were running a fever?"

Finally, ask for references such as past employers, school teachers, their own parents, friends, etc. and always be sure to check on all of them.

At some point during the interview, you should ask what the babysitter charges. Fees vary across the country, but a teen babysitter makes about $5 to $8 an hour. If you have more than one child, some sitters charge extra. And if you want the sitter to do any extra chores, such as folding laundry, be prepared to pay a little more.

Most importantly, pay attention to the reactions of the interviewee as much as the answers they give to your questions when conducting a personal interview. This will give you insight as to how sincere they are and it also shows the level of patience they have.

Important Questions to Ask During an Interview

Q: How long have you been babysitting?

Q: How much do you charge?

Q: Do you have any formal babysitting training or courses?

Q: What age of child or children do you usually watch?

Q: Have you taken care of children my child's age before?

Q: Do you know CPR or have any other training?

Q: If an emergency happened who would you call?

Q: How would you handle the children in getting them to a safe place?

Q: Are you currently babysitting for other families?

Q: What days and hours are you available?

Q: Have you ever had an emergency situation arise while babysitting? If so, how did you handle it?

Q: Do you have any younger brothers or sisters?

Q: What would you do if my child refuses to listen to you?

Q: Can you tell me about the best child you ever babysat for?

Q: How about the worst child you ever babysat for?

Q: What types of activities would you do with my children? How would you pass the time with them?

Q: What if my child told you to keep a secret? What would you do?

Q: Are there any questions that I can answer for you?

Post Interview Checklist

Use the information the applicant provided you and compare it to the checklist below.

Q: Is the applicant at least 13 years old?
Q: Is the applicant deemed responsible and reliable?
Q: Is the applicant experienced, and for how long?
Q: Did applicant provide references?
Q: Has the applicant taken a babysitter training course?
Q: Is the applicant certified in infant and child CPR?
Q: Is the applicant willing to accept your guidelines?
Q: Does the applicant understand the importance of caring for your child at all times?
Q: Does the applicant know what to do in an emergency?

Once you have determined the applicant has the basic requirements you are looking for you can then compare them to other qualified applicants who applied for the same position to get the absolute best person for the job.

Once you have made a list of possible babysitters, check their references carefully. Contact the sitter's past employers, teachers, counselors, relatives, friends, or neighbors and ask them about the sitter's qualifications specific to child care.

It is important that you take a moment now to register your copy of "A Parent's Guide to Locating Responsible Child Care." Please visit http://www.childcare-guide.info/updatedresources.html to receive access to updates, supplements and bonus gifts.

Questions to Ask Applicant's References

Q: How long have you known _(Applicants Name)_ ?

Q: What is your relationship to the applicant?

Q: In your opinion what are this applicant's strengths and weaknesses?

Q: _(Applicants Name)_ has applied as a caregiver, do you think they have the experience to look after my child?

Q: In your experience with the applicant do you believe them to be:
— Honest
— Trustworthy
— Mature
— Responsible
— Reliable

Q: Does he/she associate with persons of questionable character?

Q: Would you recommend them as a caregiver?

Q: Is there any other information you would like to provide about the applicant that you believe relates to the issues of trust and reliability?

In some states, you may be able to obtain a listing of child care services through the County Office for Children or even the police department. Look in your telephone book under "County Government" or call your local police department.

Though many young people under age 16 are capable of caring for themselves and other children, the minimum legal age when someone can be paid for working is 14. And even though someone can be paid for work at that age, you should also be aware that if your sitter is under 16 and something happens to your children during the time you are away, you will most likely be held legally responsible.

The person you choose to care for your child should be loving, responsible, honest, clean, intelligent, tolerant, patient, and caring. Make certain that they are mature, experienced, and capable individuals who truly care about the welfare and safety of children.

Choosing A Babysitter

After conducting your interviews, collecting the necessary information, completing the reference checks and police background checks you will be ready to choose a babysitter for your child.

It is important to keep in mind all the answers the potential babysitter gave you to your questions and compare that to what their references said about them. If their is a discrepancy then you can either pursue further questioning of the potential candidate by phone or rule them out altogether as a possible babysitter for your child.

For any parent having to choose a babysitter, there is always the fear of the unknown and how your child will be treated when you leave them in the care of a babysitter. If you have screened each candidate properly you will feel more comfortable and confident with your choice. You should further ensure a stable environment for your child by taking the time to discuss potential dangers your child could encounter while playing, etc.

Parents mistakenly believe that if a sitter is reliable and affectionate toward their child, that's good enough. Unfortunately, these qualities won't necessarily keep your child safe. Babysitters not only need to know what to do in an emergency, they should also be able to predict or foresee the kinds of dangers your child can get into.

Protecting your children from injury should be foremost in your mind when leaving them in someone else's care and you should openly discuss your safety concerns with the babysitter you have chosen as well as provide them with additional written instructions.

Remember, recommendations of people you know and trust are your best bet for finding a reliable and capable babysitter. You can always ask your neighbors or co-workers for referrals, or inquire at your place of worship.

You should follow your intuition and don't ever hire someone you think is mediocre because you're running out of time and if you feel that the babysitter you've hired isn't working out, don't keep her on just because you hate to fire somebody.

Remember to always put your child first!

Hiring a Nanny

Choosing a Nanny can be one of the most difficult decisions a parent can make. After all, there are so many questions you will want to have answered and so many different "if's", "and's", or "but's" you'll want closure to before making a decision, that it could very well take longer to find a suitable candidate, than what you had originally expected.

However in the end you will feel more confident and relaxed knowing that this process you are about to engage in will be worth your child's safety and learning environment.

In addition to following some of the basic steps outlined below, you should always ask for an up-to-date Resume, which will outline specific experiences and qualifications directly related to providing the services you are looking for.

Childcare Agencies

One of the most productive ways of finding a nanny is to contact and register with local childcare agencies. When you are about to register you will be asked to fill out forms which include specific information such as number of hours offered, number of children you have and their ages, any special requests or requirements from you, etc.

You should give adequate thought to answering these types of questions and include as much detail as possible because the information you provide will determine which type and qualifications of a nanny will be sent to you for an interview.

Word of Mouth

In addition to registering with your local childcare agencies, you should use word-of-mouth advertising to let others know of your needs. Friends, relatives, co-workers and neighbors could have quality leads or references to childcare providers who are looking for a position as a nanny.

Local Shops

Check with local shops and supermarkets that you frequent and ask if you can place an advertisement on their bulletin board, looking for a nanny. You can provide a brief description of the position including any specific qualifications you are looking for as well as a phone number to contact you for more specific information and setting up an interview.

Student Placement

Check with local colleges that have childcare courses or programs. Some of these courses may offer placement services for their students while they are completing their courses. Ask the college if you can be included in their placement program as well as any specific details outlining the rules and regulations for participation in such a program.

First Contact with Prospective Nanny

In most cases your first contact with a nanny will be by telephone. It is vital that you note what your first impressions of the candidate are. Be aware of how she comes across on the phone, did she strike you as quiet, reserved, loud, brash, forward, unsure or demanding?

Write down your thoughts and use them in preparation for your first interview with the prospective nanny.

Preparing for the First Interview

Prior to the first interview there are a number of matters you should attend too:

- Decide where you wish to meet her. Will it be in your home, at a convenient hotel, at an agency?
- Make a list of questions you wish to ask her.
- Have answers prepared for her in relation to wages, working hours, housework etc. These are matters which a prospective candidate interested in the position will inquire about.

The First Interview

When you first meet the prospective nanny take note of:

- Her appearance.
- How attentive is she when you ask her questions?
- Does she answer your questions without hesitation?
- Is she knowledgeable about the position she is applying for?
- Does she seem enthusiastic and interested in answering your questions honestly and completely?

Resume

You should always request an up-to-date Resume, which is a detailed list of experiences and previous employers by date. Ensure that you look for related experiences as you want performed and be sure to contact all of the former employers and references available.

Also, you should take note of any long periods of time of not working and ask them about it. These long periods or gaps may indicate a poor reference of employment which was left out.

Meet All Candidates

Be sure to meet as many candidates as possible before making your final decision. Don't be in a hurry to make a quick, hasty decision in fear of losing potentially good candidates for the position. Instead, express your interest in their abilities and let them know that they will be contacted shortly with your decision.

After every interview it is important to write down their name and any important information or special notations about how they answered your questions as well as any good or bad points about them. You will use these notes later on to determine who you will call back for a second interview.

The Second Interview — Involve the Family

During the second interview you will have the potential candidate meet your family. The interview should be conducted at your home and provide an adequate opportunity for them to answer additional questions you may have in regards to their Resume, references, and a chance to interact with your child.

This will also give your family the opportunity to later express their feelings about the candidate.

What Did Everyone Think?

Sometime during this second interview you should have the nanny interact with your child for a short period of time. This will allow you to see if there is any problems or instant dislikes, as well as positive interaction between your child and the candidate.

Before you offer the job to a candidate it is important to consult with your family and get their opinions and observations about the candidate you have chosen.

Employing a Nanny

Having decided on a candidate and offered her employment, ensure that she understands that it is on a trial basis. This trial period is usually one month and it affords you and your family an opportunity to get acquainted with the nanny you have chosen.

Trial Period

Over the course of the initial trial period there may be some minor problems such as teething, most of which can be easily remedied with some co-operation on everyone's part. If there is going to be a problem with a nanny it will often occur in these early days.

Factors that can cause problems are such issues as personal hygiene, laziness, punctuality, unwillingness to co-operate etc. If problems of this nature are not dealt with early it will be much more difficult at a later stage.

Hiring a Day Care Provider Checklist

This list is meant specifically for use when choosing professional caregivers or day care facilities that will be in charge of looking after your child on a regular basis.

First Things First

- ☐ Is the provider licensed by the state?
- ☐ If so, have you checked with the licensing agency to see if there have been any problems with compliance?
- ☐ What is the staff to child ratio?
- ☐ How have the staff members been trained? Is continuing education required or encouraged? If you are considering an individual, what is their education level? What type of training have they had?
- ☐ Does the facility have documentation of criminal background checks on all staff?
- ☐ What is the cost of childcare? What does this include?

Basic Policy

- ☐ What are the hours of operation?
- ☐ What are the policies regarding drop-off and pick-up?
- ☐ Does the provider have an open door policy?
- ☐ Is there a consent form for emergency medical care?
- ☐ Are permission forms required for transportation and medication administration?
- ☐ What are the disciplinary methods used with the children?
- ☐ What are the policies regarding breastfed infants? Will mothers be allowed to visit to feed their baby? Is there an appropriate place for this to occur?

Health & Safety

- ☐ Are the staff trained in infant and child CPR and Emergency First Aid?
- ☐ Have staff been required to have a physical and an updated TB test?
- ☐ Have you observed the staff practicing good handwashing habits?
- ☐ Are specific areas set aside for diaper changes? Are they cleaned after every use?
- ☐ Are sinks easily accessible for the children to use and are they encouraged to practice good handwashing habits?
- ☐ Are emergency procedures posted? Fire? Tornado? Flood? Earthquake?
- ☐ Are fire drills practiced?
- ☐ Are smoke detectors and fire extinguishers visible?
- ☐ Are first aid supplies easily accessible?
- ☐ Are emergency telephone numbers posted? Fire? Police? Poison Control?
- ☐ Are unused outlets covered?
- ☐ Are cabinets that hold dangerous items locked?
- ☐ Are balanced meals served? Are they age appropriate?
- ☐ Do children have access to drinking water?
- ☐ Are there pets? Do the pets comply with local health regulations? Shots updated?

Physical Environment

- ☐ Is the facility clean? Uncluttered?
- ☐ Is the environment bright and cheerful?
- ☐ Is there plenty of room for indoor and outdoor play?
- ☐ Are there designated places for various activities such as quiet time, active play, meal time?

Emotional Environment

- ☐ Do the other children seem happy and well adjusted?
- ☐ Do the children interact well with each other?
- ☐ Are babies held during meal time?
- ☐ Does the staff interact with the children appropriately?
- ☐ Does the staff listen and talk positively with the children?
- ☐ Does the staff get down on the same level with the children when interacting?
- ☐ Does the staff interact individually with the children?

Educational Environment

- ☐ Is there a TV? How much time do the children spend watching it? What programs are watched?
- ☐ What types of toys are available? Are they age appropriate? Are they cleaned regularly? If so, how?
- ☐ Are books available? Are they age appropriate?
- ☐ Can children get books and toys themselves?
- ☐ Is there a mixture of planned activities and free time? Are planned activities age appropriate?
- ☐ Are children encouraged to choose activities themselves?
- ☐ Will staff assist parents in toilet training?

Parent Involvement

- ☐ Can parents visit unannounced?
- ☐ Are written reports provided daily on the child's activities?
- ☐ Are parents encouraged to participate in special activities? (i.e. Holiday parties, field trips, etc.)

Choosing Other Child Care Programs or Facilities:

- ☐ Contact the state Department of Social Services, Community Care Licensing Division; Child Care Information and Referral Services, or other child care agencies to find out whether the program is reputable and if any complaints have been made in the past.
- ☐ Talk to other parents who use the program — ask questions about the teachers (credentials, personalities, responsiveness to parents' concerns), caretakers, facility (cleanliness, safety measures etc.) and programs offered.
- ☐ Find out if you have the right to drop in and visit the facility at any time.
- ☐ Ask if the school or center welcomes parental participation. Be alert to the degree of openness and attitude about your participation.
- ☐ Check policies regarding absences. As a safety measure, some schools will notify parents if their children are not in school.
- ☐ Never give an organization blanket permission to take your child off the premises — make sure you are informed about every outing.
- ☐ Prohibit, in writing, the release of your child to anyone without your authorization. Notify the program of who will pick up your child. Check to see if the school or program verifies phones calls stating anyone other than a designated person will be picking up your child (by calling you back at your listed number.)

The Fine Print

Once you have hired a caregiver or care center it is important to outline everything you expect them to do such as duties to be performed, amount of hours you require them for, salary, paid vacations, and sick leave. Also include parental obligations such as pay days, transportation, provide necessary emergency information, etc.

You should establish a review date within a few months, where you can sit down with the caregiver or care provider facility and express any concerns, further arrangements, things you like about their work ethic and how well they interact and care for your child. You can also use this time to fine-tune the agreement and add or delete any other special arrangements.

This review will also be used to determine if you no longer wish to employ this particular caregiver or facility. If you choose this route, ensure that you have alternate childcare established so this won't cause a problem. It's also important to let the caregiver or facilitator know exactly why you don't require their services any longer. Sometimes it could be due to your changing situation and not their performance.

It is important that you take a moment now to register your copy of "A Parent's Guide to Locating Responsible Child Care." Please visit http://www.childcare-guide.info/updatedresources.html to receive access to updates, supplements and bonus gifts.

Take the time to let your babysitter know your child care expectations before you leave your home. If you'd prefer that the sitter not leave the house with your child, make that clear. If the phone and any visitors are off limits, don't hesitate to discuss the restrictions with the sitter.

— CHAPTER THREE —
Quick Reference Kit

All child care providers must realize that their only job is caring for your child while in their care.

It's always a good idea to remind your child care provider if at any time they feel they cannot handle something, make the phone call for help. This should be especially emphasized to younger babysitters at home alone with your child.

The following chapter is designed to give your babysitter all the necessary information they will require should an emergency arise. It is important for you to fill out this information accurately and completely for your child's benefit — it could save their life!

By giving this information to your babysitter you will make them feel more confident and relaxed, should a situation occur. It is also important to take the time to go over the information you have provided with your babysitter and any questions or concerns should be addressed at that time.

Babysitter Quick Reference Kit

Write down where you will be and include the address and phone number.

Write down important phone numbers such as

— Your own phone number and address
— Your family doctor's name and phone number
— Poison Control Center phone number
— Neighbor's name and phone number
— Friend's name and phone number
— Relative's name and phone number

Important information about your child, such as

— Age
— Medical history
— Current medications
— Allergies

Location of First Aid Kit

Location of Fire Extinguisher

— Should a fire occur be calm
— Locate the children
— Stay low to the floor
— Touch closed doors with the back of your hand
— DO NOT open the door if it is hot.
— Quickly and safely exit the house at the nearest exit

— Go to the neighbor's house located at _____.
— Call 9-1-1
— Our home address is _____.

Safety Precautions

Ensure that you know where the children are in the house at all times.

Adequately supervise the children.

Check on children frequently.

Ensure safety of children at all times. If you are unsure about something, don't let them do it.

Keep the doors locked at all times, and DO NOT unlock the door to strangers.

If someone calls DO NOT tell them you are there alone.

Ensure the children get to bed on time.

Check the temperature of all heated foods and liquids before giving it to the children.

Never leave young children alone on changing tables, not even for a second.

Make sure all safety gates are up and in place properly.

Ensure that all harmful chemicals, materials, vitamins, cosmetics are out of the child's reach.

If you suspect a child of ingesting something harmful, call the poison control center or family doctor immediately and follow their instructions.

Beware of choking hazards. Do not give children under age 6 hard or round foods. Check the floor for small objects. Never let children wear clothing with items around their necks while using playground equipment.

Never leave a child alone in the bathtub — even in a bath ring or similar device. Empty all sinks, tubs, buckets and containers immediately after use. Store buckets upside down.

Keep cribs safe by removing all soft bedding and placing infants on their backs to sleep. Never hang anything on or above a crib with string or ribbon. Never place a crib near a window.

Parent Instructions

- Show the babysitter where emergency exits, smoke detectors, and fire extinguishers are located. Demonstrate how to enable and disable security systems and alarms.
- Show the sitter where you keep the door keys in case your child locks herself inside a room.
- Let the sitter know of any special problems your child may have, such as an allergy to bee stings, certain foods, or household products, or the need for medication at a specific time (the directions for which should be clearly explained and written down). Show the sitter where first-aid items are kept.
- Teach your child the meaning of 9-1-1 and how to call for help, so that if something happens to your babysitter, your child knows what to do.
- Take the time to let your babysitter know your child care expectations before you leave your home. If you'd prefer that the sitter not leave the house with your child, make that clear. If the phone and any visitors are off limits, don't hesitate to discuss the restrictions with the sitter.

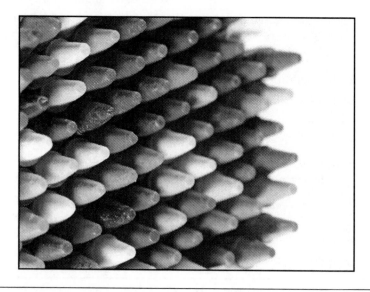

Additional Safety Points

- Don't give child any medicine without parents' written instructions.
- Don't leave the child alone in the house or yard, even for a minute.
- Don't leave the child unattended whenever they are near water. Infants and small children can drown in only a few inches of water.
- Don't feed the child under 4 years old nuts, popcorn, hard candy, raw carrots, or any hard, smooth foods that can block the windpipe and cause choking. Foods such as hot dogs or grapes should be chopped into small pieces.
- Don't let the child play with plastic bags, latex balloons, coins, or other small objects they could choke on.
- Don't let the child play near stairs, windows, stoves, or electrical outlets.
- Don't have the babysitter's friends visit the house or be around the children.

Child Care Center Helpful Reminders

This section deals with taking your child to a care provider outside of your home. Most of the forms you had filled out while enrolling your child in the child care center will be on file and should include such things as

- Your child's medical history
- Any allergies
- How you can be reached, your phone number and where you work
- Relative's phone numbers
- Neighbor's phone numbers
- Family doctor's name and phone number
- Food allergies or restrictions

If any of this important information changes, such as medications, allergies, etc. it is imperative to let the childcare facility know so they can update your child's file.

You should have also checked to see if the child care center has the proper insurance and the correct amount of staff to children ratio.

If, at any time while dropping your child off, you feel uncomfortable about the qualifications of the staff you should not leave your child there.

Talk with the facilitator often about any concerns, even when things are going well tell them at the center, they should always welcome your feedback.

If the center is planning any trips away from the childcare center it is important that they get your permission, in writing, ahead of time. Most often this will be done in the form of a flyer or letter sent home with the child for you to read, sign and deliver back to the school.

Again, if you feel uncomfortable about your child being away from the center without you being there, it is important to talk with the facilitator immediately to express your concern. Alternate arrangements may in fact be made for those children staying behind.

Child Care Safety Checklist:

☐ **Cribs** — Make sure cribs meet current national safety standards and are in good condition. Look for a certification safety seal. Older cribs may not meet current standards. Crib slats should be no more than 2-3/8" apart, and mattresses should fit snugly.

This can prevent strangulation and suffocation associated with older cribs and mattresses that are too small.

☐ **Soft Bedding** — Be sure that no pillows, soft bedding, or comforters are used when you put babies to sleep. Babies should be put to sleep on their backs in a crib with a firm, flat mattress.

This can help reduce Sudden Infant Death Syndrome (SIDS) and suffocation related to soft bedding.

☐ **Playground Surfacing** — Look for safe surfacing on outdoor playgrounds — at least 12 inches of wood chips, mulch, sand or pea gravel, or mats made of safety-tested rubber or rubber-like materials. These materials help protect against injuries from falls, especially head injuries.

☐ **Playground Maintenance** — Check playground surfacing and equipment regularly to make sure they are maintained in good condition. This can help prevent injuries, especially from falls.

❑ **Safety Gates** — Be sure that safety gates are used to keep children away from potentially dangerous areas, especially stairs. Safety gates can protect against many hazards, especially falls.

❑ **Window Blinds and Curtain Cords** — Be sure mini-blinds and Venetian blinds do not have looped cords. Check that vertical blinds, continuous looped blinds, and drapery cords have tension or tie-down devices to hold the cords tight.

These safety devices can prevent strangulation in the loops of window blind and curtain cords.

- Safeguard your windows with window guards or window stops.
- Install *window guards* to prevent children from falling out of windows. (For windows on the 6th floor and below, install window guards that adults and older children can open easily in case of fire.)
- Install *window stops* so that windows open no more than 4 inches.
- Never depend on screens to keep children from falling out of windows.
- Whenever possible, open windows from the top — not the bottom.
- Keep furniture away from windows, to discourage children from climbing near windows.

☐ **Clothing Drawstrings** — Be sure there are no drawstrings around the hood and neck of children's outerwear clothing. Other types of clothing fasteners, like snaps, zippers, or hook and loop fasteners (such as Velcro), should be used.

Drawstrings can catch on playground and other equipment and can strangle young children.

☐ **Recalled Products** — Check that no recalled products are being used and that a current list of recalled children's products is readily visible.

Recalled products pose a threat of injury or death. Displaying a list of recalled products will remind caretakers and parents to remove or repair potentially dangerous children's toys and products.

It is important that you take a moment now to register your copy of "A Parent's Guide to Locating Responsible Child Care." Please visit http://www.childcare-guide.info/updatedresources.html to receive access to updates, supplements and bonus gifts.

Percentage of Child Care Centers With Safety Hazard — The chart refers to four types of licensed child care settings that were visited: Federal General Services Administration child care centers, non-profit centers, in-home settings, and for-profit centers.

	Overall	GSA	Non-Profit	In-Home	For-Profit
Unsafe Cribs	8%	10%	15%	8%	0%
Soft Bedding Present	19%	42%	21%	8%	14%
Playground Safety: Unsafe Surfacing	24%	5%	18%	46%	17%
Playground Safety: Poor Maintenance	27%	11%	24%	33%	31%
Safety Gates Not Used	13%	6%	8%	21%	13%
Blind Cord Loops Present	26%	22%	31%	26%	20%
Drawstrings on Children's Outerwear	38%	30%	45%	26%	47%
Recalled Products in Use	5%	4%	5%	6%	4%

Safety Tips For Sleeping Babies

If your baby is under 12 months old, you can help prevent SIDS *(Sudden Infant Death Syndrome)*, suffocation, and strangulation by following these three tips:

- Place your baby to sleep on his or her back.
- Remove all soft bedding from the crib.
- Put your baby to sleep in a safe crib.

Why follow these tips?

- Babies who sleep on their backs have a much lower risk of dying from SIDS and suffocation. African American babies die from SIDS at more than twice the rate of other babies.
- A baby can suffocate from soft bedding in a crib. Be sure to remove all pillows, quilts, comforters, and sheepskins from your crib.
- A safe crib is the best place for your baby to sleep. Make sure your crib has:
  — no missing or broken hardware and slats no more than 2-3/8" apart
  — no corner posts over 1/16" high
  — no cut-out designs in the headboard or footboard
  — a firm, tight-fitting mattress
  — a safety certification seal (on new cribs)

Toy Safety Tips

Under 3 Years Old — Children under 3 tend to put everything in their mouths. Avoid buying toys intended for older children which may have small parts that pose a choking danger.

Never let children of any age play with un-inflated or broken balloons because of the choking danger.

Avoid marbles, balls, and games with balls, that have a diameter of 1.75 inches or less. These products also pose a choking hazard to young children.

Children at this age pull, prod and twist toys. Look for toys that are well-made with tightly secured eyes, noses and other parts.

Avoid toys that have sharp edges and points.

Ages 3 Through 5 — Avoid toys that are constructed with thin, brittle plastic that might easily break into small pieces or leave jagged edges.

Look for household art materials, including crayons and paint sets, marked with the designation "ASTM D-4236." This means the product has been reviewed by a toxicologist and, if necessary, labeled with cautionary information.

Teach older children to keep their toys away from their younger brothers and sisters.

Ages 6 Through 12 — For all children, adults should check toys periodically for breakage and potential hazards. Damaged or dangerous toys should be repaired or thrown away.

If buying a toy gun, be sure the barrel, or the entire gun, is brightly colored so that it's not mistaken for a real gun.

If you buy a bicycle for any age child, buy a helmet too, and make sure the child wears it.

Teach all children to put toys away when they're finished playing so they don't trip over them or fall on them.

Read The Label ...

The U. S. Consumer Product Safety Commission **[http://www.cpsc.gov/ kids/kidsafety/index.html]** requires toy manufacturers to meet stringent safety standards and to label certain toys that could be a hazard for younger children.

Look for labels that give age recommendations and use that information as a guide.

Labels on toys that state "not recommended for children under three ... contains small parts," are labeled that way because they may pose a choking hazard to children under three.

Toys should be developmentally appropriate to suit the skills, abilities and interests of the child.

Shopping for toys during the holidays can be exciting and fun, but it can also be frustrating. There can be thousands of toys to choose from in one store, and it's important to choose the right toy for the right age child. Toys that are meant for older children can be dangerous for younger children.

Last year, an estimated 140,700 children were treated in U.S. hospital emergency rooms after toy-related incidents and 13 children died.

It is important that you take a moment now to register your copy of
"A Parent's Guide to Locating Responsible Child Care." Please visit
http://www.childcare-guide.info/updatedresources.html
to receive access to updates, supplements and bonus gifts.

False complaints from a child about sexual abuse is quite rare. If a child tells you about any form of sexual abuse, whether or not it involves touching, treat them with compassion and respect.

— CHAPTER FOUR —
Child Abuse

Although statistics of child abuse related deaths will vary from agency to agency due to non-reporting of the abuse and inconsistent documented incidents, resulting in inaccurate data and clear identification of child deaths linked to child abuse, it continues to be a wide spread problem through our economic, social, racial, ethnic and religious boundaries with a case being reported approximately every ten seconds or three million reported cases every year, with girls being sexually abused three times more often than boys.

Children are hurt or abused by a parent, guardian, relative, family friend, babysitter, or other childcare provider who are familiar and most often trusted by the child.

More than three children die everyday, as a direct result of child abuse stemming from their own homes. Of these deaths, more than three-quarters of child victims were under the age of five and thirty-eight percent were under the age of one.

Many forms of abuse most often occur with some regularity and even increase in severity and frequency over a period of time. Over ninety percent of children under the age of twelve who are sexually abused know their attacker, and one of every seven victims of reported sexual abuse are under the age of six.

Children four years old and younger die from child abuse and neglect more often than from accidental falls, drowning, choking on food, suffocation, fires in the home, or motor vehicle accidents.

Victims of child abuse often grow up repeating their learned violent behavior and have a greater risk of abusing their own children and continuing the cycle of abuse.

Child Abuse

Child abuse is defined as any form of abuse that inhibits or restricts the child's mental and physical abilities which denies the child's right to grow and maximize their potential in a healthy environment for which there is no "reasonable" explanation and includes non-accidental physical injury, neglect, sexual molestation, and emotional abuse.

Abuse includes:
- Physical injury that is inflicted on a child other than accidental means by another person.
- Cruelty or unjustifiable punishment of a child.
- Cruel or inhumane punishment or injury.
- General and severe neglect.
- Sexual abuse, including assault and exploitation.

Abuse of all of the above reflects out-of-home care such as foster homes, administrator or employee of a school, residential home, or other agencies.

Indications of Child Abuse
When The Child ...
- Shows a sudden change in behavior or performance in school.
- Has not received medical or emotional help for problems brought to the parents' attention.

- Has learning difficulties that cannot be attributed to specific physical or psychological causes.
- Is always watchful, fearful, or apprehensive.
- Lacks adult supervision.
- Is overly compliant to instructions in fear of retaliation.
- Arrives at school early, stays late, and does not want to go home.

When The Parent ...
- Shows little or no concern for their child, and rarely responds to school's request for information, conferences, or home visits.
- Denies the existence of problems with the child, or blames the child for such problems.
- Allows or even requests the caregiver to use harsh physical discipline if the child misbehaves.
- Sees the child as entirely bad, worthless, or burdensome.
- Demands perfection, or a level of physical or academic performance that is unrealistic for the child or that the child cannot achieve.
- Looks primarily to the child for attention, satisfaction and care of emotional needs.

The Child and Parent ...
- Rarely touch or look at each other.
- Consider their relationship as being entirely negative.
- State to others or to one another that they do not like each other.

Physical Abuse

Physical abuse is defined as any act which results in non-accidental injury, including excessive and unjustified corporal punishment inflicted by, or allowed to be inflicted by, responsible persons. Corporal punishment is the infliction of cruel or inhumane physical injury resulting in trauma.

Indications of Physical Abuse
When The Child ...
- Has bruises, burns, abrasions, lacerations, swelling, broken bones or black eyes not caused by accidental means.

- Has faded bruises or other marks noticeable after an absence from school.
- Has belt buckle, cord, hanger, paddle marks, hand prints, bite marks, or pinches present.
- States injury was caused by abuse and or reports the injury as being inflicted by a parent or another caregiver.
- Has an injury unusual for a specific age group.
- Has a history of previous and or re-occurring injuries.
- Has unexplainable or conflicting explanations for reasons of injury.
- Seems frightened of parents, protests or cries when it is time to go home from school.
- Shrinks at the approach of adults.
- Is excessively passive, compliant, or fearful.

When The Parent or Other Caregiver ...
- Attempts to hide the child's injuries.
- Offers conflicting, unconvincing, or no explanation for the child's injury.
- Uses harsh physical discipline with the child.
- Describes the child in negative ways

Emotional Abuse

Emotional abuse is defined as a wilful and or uncontrollable repetition or infliction of mental suffering to a child which often includes yelling, blaming, belittling, name-calling, prolonged ignoring, refusing to attend to the child's emotional needs.

Indications of Emotional Abuse Include

When a Child ...

- Shows extremes in behavior — overly compliant or demanding; extremely passive or aggressive.
- Is isolated or withdrawn and or argues, fights or gets into trouble to let out their anger.
- Is inappropriately "adult" (i.e. parenting other children).
- Is inappropriately infantile (i.e. frequently rocking or head-banging).
- Behind or delayed in physical or emotional development.
- Shows difficulty making and keeping friends.
- Has attempted or contemplating suicide.
- Reports lack of attachment to their parent.

When The Parent or Other Caregiver ...

- Constantly blame, belittle, or berates the child.
- Overtly rejects the child.
- Is unconcerned about the child and or refuses offers of help for the child's problems.

Neglect

Neglect of a child encompasses the negligent treatment or maltreatment of a child by a parent or caregiver under circumstances indicating harm or threatened to harm the child's health and or welfare. Neglect can also include severe malnutrition and endangerment of a child's body and or health. Physical injury need not occur for child neglect to be reported.

The types of neglect include general neglect and severe neglect, which differ from each other.

General Neglect

General neglect is the deprivation of adequate food, clothing, shelter, medical care, or supervision where no physical or emotional injury to the child has occurred.

Severe Neglect

Severe neglect is the failure to protect a child from endangerment both physically and mentally, and failing to allow growth in these areas.

Indications of Neglect Include

When a Child ...

- Is frequently absent from school.
- Lacks adequate medical care, dental care, immunizations, glasses, etc.
- Is consistently dirty and or lacks proper hygiene.
- Is inadequately dressed for weather conditions.
- Is always hungry, begs or steals food or money from classmates.
- Is always sleepy, groggy or tired.
- States there is no one at home to provide care or supervision.
- Indicates that conditions in the home are extremely unsafe and or unsanitary.

When The Parent or Other Caregiver ...

- Appears to be indifferent to the child and their needs.
- Is uninterested toward the care of the child.
- Seems depressed.
- Behaves irrationally.
- Is abusing alcohol or other drugs.

Sexual Abuse

Sexual abuse is defined as molestation, lewd touching, any form of sexual assault, incest, sexual exploitation of minors, and the physical and or emotional involvement of a child in sexual activities which can occur between an adult and child or adolescent and child.

Further, child sexual abuse also includes acts of nudity, disrobing, genital exposure, observation of the child (these do not always involve touching, skin-to-skin or genital contact), kissing, fondling, masturbation, oral-genital contact, digital penetration, vaginal or anal intercourse, and child pornography.

Child sexual exploitation defined as the depiction of a minor engaged in obscene acts and the employment or encouragement of a child to engage in prostitution or to pose in live and or photographed sexual performances.

Indications of Sexual Abuse Include

When a Child ... Reports sexual activities to a trusted person.

A child may be too frightened to report sexual abuse and may make indirect comments about the activity or exhibit a variety of physical and behavioral signals such as:

- A detailed and age-inappropriate understanding of sexual behavior.
- Demonstrates sophisticated or unusual sexual knowledge or behavior.
- Expresses affection in ways inappropriate for the child's age.
- Wears torn, stained, or bloodied underclothing.
- Suffers vaginal and or rectal bleeding, pain, itching, swollen genitals, or vaginal discharge.
- Becomes pregnant or contracts a sexually-transmitted disease, particularly if very young.
- Has difficulty walking or sitting.
- Suddenly refuses to change for extra-curricular classes or negates participation in physical activities.
- Begins to fail in school, starts delinquent or disruptive behavior.
- Exhibits behavioral changes such as hostility, anxiety, withdrawal, fearfulness, or crying without provocation.
- Returns to more infantile behavior, such as bed-wetting, thumb sucking, or excessive crying.
- Has significant changes in appetite.
- Recurrent nightmares, disturbed sleep patterns, and even fear of the dark.
- Has fear or intense dislike at being left somewhere or with someone.

- Runs away.
- Is the victim of other forms of abuse.

When Parent or Other Caregiver ...
- Is unduly protective of the child.
- Severely limits the child's contact with other children.
- Is secretive and isolated.
- Describes marital difficulties involving family power struggles or sexual relations.

What Do I Do If I Suspect My Child Has Been Sexually Abused?

False complaints from a child about sexual abuse is quite rare. If a child tells you about any form of sexual abuse, whether or not it involves touching, treat them with compassion and respect.

- Believe the child.
- Assure the child that you will protect them.
- Commend the child for telling you about the experience.
- Support the child. Assure them that they are NOT at fault or in any way responsible for the incident. Help the child to remove self-blame.
- Control your own reactions. Your acceptance is important to the child who has sought you out.
- Report the suspected abuse to the police and or a social service agency before going to the school or program where the child says something happened to confront them with your concerns.
- Find a specialized agency that can assist you and evaluate sexual abuse victims, such as the Department of Child Services, a hospital, community mental health program or sexual abuse treatment center.
- Seek medical attention from a physician with experience and training in detecting and recognizing sexual abuse. Children's hospitals and community sexual abuse treatment programs may provide referrals.
- Talk with other parents to ascertain if their child has exhibited similar behavior or physical changes and symptoms.
- Take action! It is important because other children may be or will continue to be at risk if nothing is done.

Creating a Positive Atmosphere

It can be quite difficult at times to communicate within your family, especially for working parents. Good communication within your family is the key to keeping your child safe from all forms of abuse. It is up to you, as a parent, to create an atmosphere in which your children are not afraid to confide in you.

- Listen to your child and talk with them every day. Encourage them to share their concerns.

- Learn about your children's activities and feelings so that changes will be more apparent to you.

- Be alert for any changes in personality, attitude, behavior, or physical problems.

- Teach your child about strangers and discuss with them whom they can trust.

- Teach your child at an early age that it is all right to say "no," even to an adult, in certain situations and to tell someone about the incident.

- Encourage your child to keep telling until someone helps them. An unprepared child may be too confused or ashamed to admit that abuse has taken place, especially sexual abuse.

- Teach your child which touches are good and which touches are bad. Explain that they have the right to say "no" to anyone who might try to touch them, and that if they are confused if it is a good touch or a bad touch, they should say "NO" and tell someone.

- Tell your child that someone they know and trust or love (such as a relative, family friend, babysitter, caregiver, teacher or neighbor) might try to touch them inappropriately, get them to do something they don't want to do, or be abusive toward them. Explain that most people do not do these things and they should tell you immediately if this happens.

- Explain to your child that some people may try to hurt them and tell them that what they are doing is a secret. Some people even threaten the child by saying their parents will be hurt if the child tells the secret. Tell your child that anyone who does this is wrong.

- Make sure your child knows you want to be told about someone who does something hurtful or confusing to them, like touching them, giving them gifts or asking to take a picture of your child.
- Re-assure your child that they have done anything wrong and won't be blamed for whatever an adult does to them.

Words that help:
- I love you.
- You're very special to me.
- I'm so lucky to have you.
- You're a great kid!
- Good job!
- You can do it!
- I believe in you!
- Thank you for being patient while I had to ___.
- Tell me about your day.
- Let's talk about what's upsetting you.
- I'm sorry.

Leaving Your Child With Another Adult

At some point in a child's life their parents will leave them in the care of another adult and some parents even have regular arrangements with friends or family members to care for their child while at work. Children who spend time with other adults who love and care for them can in fact help your child develop confidence and security.

Parents must feel confident about leaving their child in the care of other adults, even if they are relatives and must know the level of care their child is receiving.

It is important that you take a moment now to register your copy of "A Parent's Guide to Locating Responsible Child Care." Please visit http://www.childcare-guide.info/updatedresources.html to receive access to updates, supplements and bonus gifts.

To help make a good choice, ask yourself these important questions:

- Do I trust this person to take good care of my child?
- Will my child be happy in the care of this person?
- Is this person capable of caring for a child of this age?
- Will there be things for my child to do at this persons place?
- Does this person have any problems like health related problems, other commitments, abuse of drugs or alcohol, that might get in the way of their giving my child the care they need?
- Is this a safe place and atmosphere for my child?

By taking the necessary steps to ensure that you have the absolute best child care available for your child you will feel much more relaxed when you leave your child in the care of the provider of your choice.

— CHAPTER FIVE —
Putting It All Together

How To Screen Any Child Care Provider

Screening anyone is a matter of asking the right kinds of questions. You must first develop your reasons why you want to screen someone. What do you want to find out about that individual?

The Step-By-Step Process

I have outlined the things you need to be aware of when selecting a child care provider, in this book.

The best way to go about using this book is to first determine which kind of child care provider you are looking for … Will it be a day care or a live-in nanny …?

Once you know what you're looking for you need to go through this book again and concentrate on those chapters that reflect your needs.

Make as many questions that come to mind and I'm sure you'll have plenty more as you start conducting interviews.

You'll definitely want to know this person's experience or if choosing a daycare, you'll want to know all the employees and their experiences.

As well you'll also want to ask about security issues and procedures the day care facility has in place if a child goes missing.

Don't be afraid to ask the tough questions and don't allow anyone to make you feel rushed. You keep asking questions and keep interviewing other people and places until you feel comfortable.

Making Your Final Selection

After you have interviewed several people and several day care providers you'll want to assemble your notes and compare them.

Once you make your final decision go back to your initial list and make a second choice. This way if your first selection does not do an adequate job in your eyes or something unforeseen happens you'll have an immediate backup provider, in most cases, just a phone call away.

CONCLUSION

It is important to arrange your child care needs well in advance so that you can prepare your child for interaction with other children as well as other adults when you are not present.

It is also important for your child to understand why you are sending them out of the home or bringing someone else into your home to care for them. Children don't understand why you have to work or be away from them.

Utilize the forms that have been included with this publication to make the screening process for child care as accurate as possible. Remember that you are conducting this process for the benefit of your child.

By taking the necessary steps to ensure that you have the absolute best child care available for your child you will feel much more relaxed when you leave your child in the care of the provider of your choice.

It is important that you take a moment now to register your copy of
"A Parent's Guide to Locating Responsible Child Care." Please visit
http://www.childcare-guide.info/updatedresources.html
to receive access to updates, supplements and bonus gifts.

National Child Care Programs

Visit **http://www.childcare-guide.info/updatedresources.html**
to receive access to an updated list of resources.

National Child Care Center Information:
http://nccic.acf.hhs.gov/statedata/statepro/

Child Care Lookup by State:
http://www.childcarelookup.com/stateagencies.html

Child and Dependent Care Tax Credit
[http://www.irs.gov/newsroom/article/0,,id=106189,00.html]

Head Start Program
[http://www.acf.hhs.gov/programs/hsb/]

Federal Food Programs
[http://www.frac.org/html/federal_food_programs/programs/cacfp.html]

CHILD CARE and DEVELOPMENT STATE RESOURCES & FUNDS DIRECTORY

This directory will give you information on where to look for subsidies for your child care requirements. Listed by state you will find these links to be most helpful and in most cases you can apply for the necessary funding online.

Alabama
Alabama Department of
  Human Resources
Child Day Care Partnerships
50 North Ripley Street
Montgomery, AL 36104
Phone: 334-242-9513
Fax: 334-242-0513

Alaska
Alaska Dept. of Education and
  Early Development
Division of Early Development
619 E. Ship Creek Ave, Suite 230
Anchorage, AK 99501-2341
Phone: 907-269-4607
Fax: 907-269-4635

Arizona

Arizona Dept. of Economic Security
Child Care Administration
1789 W. Jefferson, 801A
Phoenix, AZ 85007
Phone: 602-542-4244
Fax: 602-542-4197

Arkansas

Arkansas Department of Human
Services
Division of Child Care and Early
Education
101 East Capitol, Suite 106
Little Rock AR 72201
Phone: 501-682-4891
Fax: 501-682-4897 or 501-682-2317

California

California State Dept. of Education
Child Development Division
560 J Street, Suite 220
Sacramento, CA 95814-4785
Phone: 916-324-8296
Fax: 916-323-6853

Colorado

Colorado Dept. of Human Services
Division of Child Care
1575 Sherman Street
Denver, CO 80203-1714
Phone: 303-866-5958 or 800-799-5876
Fax: 303-866-4453

Connecticut

Connecticut Department of Social
Services
Family Services/ Child Care Team
25 Sigourney Street 10th Floor
Hartford, CT 06106-5033
Phone: 860-424-5006
Fax: 860-951-2996

Delaware

Delaware Dept. of Health & Social
Services
Lewis Building B Herman Holloway
Campus
1901 N. DuPont Highway, P.O. Box
906
New Castle, DE 19720
Phone: 302-577-4880
Fax: 302-577-4405

District of Columbia

DC Dept. of Human Services
Office of Early Childhood
Development
Commission on Social Service
717 14th Street NW #730
Washington, DC 20005
Phone: 202-727-1839
Fax: 202-727-7228

Florida

Florida Partnership for School
Readiness
Holland Building, Room 251
600 S. Calhoun Street
Tallahassee, FL 32399-0001
Phone: 850-922-4200
Fax: 850-922-5188

Georgia

Georgia Dept. of Human Resources
Child Care and Parent Services
Two Peachtree Street NW, Suite 21-293
Atlanta, GA 30303
Phone: 404-657-3434
Fax: 404-657-3489

Hawaii
Hawaii Department of Human Services
Benefit, Employment, and Support
  Services Division
820 Mililani Street, Suite 606, Haseko
  Center
Honolulu, HI 96813
Phone: 808-586-7050
Fax: 808-586-5229

Idaho
Idaho Dept. of Health and Welfare
Division of Welfare
Bureau of Policy
450 West State Street 6th Floor
P.O. Box 83720
Boise, ID 83720-0036
Phone: 208-334-5818
Fax: 208-334-4916

Illinois
Illinois Department of Human Services
Office of Child Care and Family
  Services
300 Iles Park Place, Suite 270
Springfield,, IL 62762
Phone: 217-785-2559
Fax: 217-524-6030

Indiana
Indiana Family & Social Services
  Administration
Bureau of Child Development/Division
  of Family & Children
402 W. Washington Street, W392
Indianapolis, IN 46204
Phone: 317-234-2250 or 800-441-7837
Fax: 317-232-4490

Iowa
Iowa Department of Human Services
Division of ACFS
Bureau of Family and Community
  Support
Hoover State Office Building — 5th
  Floor
Des Moines, IA 50319-0114
Phone: 515-281-4357
Fax: 515-281-4597

Kansas
Kansas Dept. of Social & Rehab.
  Services
Child Care and Early Childhood
  Development
915 SW Harrison, 5th Floor South
Topeka, KS 66612-1570
Phone: 785-296-3314
Fax: 785-368-8159

Kentucky
Kentucky Cabinet for Families and
  Children
Department for Community Based
  Services
Division of Child Care
275 East Main Street, 3E-B6
Frankfort, KY 40621
Phone: 502-564-2524 or 800-421-1903
Fax: 502-564-3464

Louisiana
Louisiana Department of Social
  Services
Child Care Assistance Program
Office of Family Support, FIND Work/
  Child Care Division
P.O. Box 91193
Baton Rouge, LA 70821-9193
Phone: 225-342-9106
Fax: 225-342-9111

Maine
Maine Department of Human Services
Office of Child Care and Head Start
11 State House Station, 221 State
  Street
Augusta, ME 04333-0011
Phone: 207-287-5060
Fax: 207-287-5031

Maryland
Maryland Department of Human
  Resources
Child Care Administration
311 W. Saratoga Street 1st Floor
Baltimore, MD 21201
Phone: 410-767-7128
Fax: 410-333-8699

Massachusetts
Massachusetts Office of Child Care
  Services
One Ashburton Place, Room 1105
Boston, MA 02108
Phone: 617-626-2000
Fax: 617-626-2028

Michigan
Michigan Family Independence Agency
Child Development and Care Division
235 South Grand Ave., Suite 1302
P.O. Box 30037
Lansing, MI 48909-7537
Phone: 517-373-0356
Fax: 517-241-7843

Minnesota
Minnesota Dept. of Children, Families
  & Learning
1500 Highway 36 West
Roseville, MN 55113-4266
Phone: 651-582-8562
Fax: 651-582-8496

Mississippi
Mississippi Department of Human
  Services
Office for Children and Youth
750 North State Street
P. O. Box 352
Jackson, MS 39205-0352
Phone: 601-359-4555
Fax: 601-359-4422

Missouri
Missouri Division of Family Services
615 Howerton Court
P.O. Box 88
Jefferson City, MO 65103
Phone: 573-522-1137
Fax: 573-526-4837

Montana
Montana Department of Public Health
  and Human Services
Human and Community Services
  Division
Early Childhood Services Bureau
P.O. Box 202952
Helena, MT 59620-2952
Phone: 406-444-1828
Fax: 406-444-2547

Nebraska
Nebraska Department of Health and
  Human Services System
Child Care
P.O. Box 95044
Lincoln, NE 68509
Phone: 402-471-9370
Fax: 402-471-9597

Nevada

Nevada Department of Human
 Resources
Welfare Division
2527 N. Carson Street
1470 E. College Parkway
Carson City, NV 89706
Phone: 775-687-1172
Fax: 775-687-1079

New Hampshire

New Hampshire Dept. of Health &
 Human Services
Division for Children, Youth &
 Families
Bureau of Child Development
129 Pleasant Street
Concord, NH 03301-3857
Phone: 603-271-8153
Fax: 603-271-4729

New Jersey

New Jersey Dept. of Human Services
Division of Family Development
P.O. Box 716
Trenton, NJ 08625
Phone: 609-588-2163
Fax: 609-588-3369

New Mexico

New Mexico Dept. of Children, Youth
 and Families
Child Care Services Bureau
PERA Building, Room 111
PO Drawer 5160
Santa Fe, NM 87502-5160
Phone: 505-827-9932
Fax: 505-827-7361

New York

New York State Department of Family
 Assistance
Office of Children and Family Services
Bureau Of Early Childhood Services
40 North Pearl Street 11B
Albany, NY 12243
Phone: 518-474-9324
Fax: 518-474-9617

North Carolina

North Carolina Dept. of Health and
 Human Services
Division of Child Development
2201 Mail Service Center
Raleigh, NC 27699-2201
Phone: 919-662-4499
Fax: 919-662-4568

North Dakota

North Dakota Department of Human
 Services
Office of Economic Assistance
State Capitol Judicial Wing
600 East Boulevard Avenue
Bismarck, ND 58505-0250
Phone: 701-328-2332
Fax: 701-328-1060

Ohio

Ohio Department of Job and Family
 Services
Bureau of Child Care Services
255 East Main Street, 3rd Floor
Columbus, OH 43215
Phone: 614-466-1043
Fax: 614-728-6803

Oklahoma

Oklahoma Dept. of Human Services
Division of Child Care
Sequoyah Memorial Office Building
P.O. Box 25352
Oklahoma City, OK 73125-0352
Phone: 405-521-3561 or 800-347-2276
Fax: 405-522-2564

Oregon

Oregon Department of Employment
Child Care Division
875 Union Street NE
Salem, OR 97311
Phone: 503-947-1400
Fax: 503-947-1428

Pennsylvania

Pennsylvania Department of Public
  Welfare
Office of Children, Youth and Families
Box 2675
Harrisburg, PA 17105-2675
Phone: 717-787-8691
Fax: 717-787-1529

Puerto Rico

Puerto Rico Department of the Family
Administration for Families and
  Children
Child Care and Development Program
Avenida Ponce de Leon, PDA.2, San
  Juan
Apartado 15091
San Juan, PR 00902-5091
Phone: 787-722-8157
Fax: 787-723-5357

Rhode Island

Rhode Island Department of Human
  Services
Louis Pasteur Bldg. #57
600 New London Avenue
Cranston, RI 02920
Phone: 401-462-3415
Fax: 401-462-6878

South Carolina

South Carolina Department of Health
  and Human Services
Bureau of Community Services
Child Care and Development Services
P.O. Box 8206
1801 Main Street 8th Floor
Columbia, SC 29202-8206
Phone: 803-898-2570
Fax: 803-898-4510

South Dakota

South Dakota Department of Social
  Services
Child Care Services
700 Governors Drive
Pierre, SD 57501-2291
Phone: 605-773-4766 or 800-227-3020
Fax: 605-773-6834

Tennessee

Tennessee Department of Human
  Services
Child Care Services
Citizens Plaza - 14th Floor
400 Deaderick Street
Nashville, TN 37248-9600
Phone: 615-313-4770
Fax: 615-532-9956

Texas

Texas Workforce Commission
Child Care Management
101 East 15th Street Suite 440T
Austin, TX 78778-0001
Phone: 512-936-0474
Fax: 512-463-5067

Utah

Utah Department of Workforce
  Services
Office of Child Care
140 East 300 South
Salt Lake City, UT 84111
Phone: 801-526-4341
Fax: 801-526-4349

Vermont

Vermont Department of Social and
  Rehabilitation Services
Agency for Human Services
Child Care Services Division
103 South Main Street 2nd Floor
Waterbury, VT 05671-2401
Phone: 802-241-3110
Fax: 802-241-1220

Virgin Islands

Virgin Islands Dept. of Human Services
Knud Hansen Complex Bldg. A
1303 Hospital Ground
Charlotte Amalie, 00802
Phone: 340-774-0930 ext. 4141
Fax: 340-774-3466 or 340-774-7773

Virginia

Virginia Department of Social Services
Child Day Care
730 E. Broad St.
Richmond, VA 23219-1849
Phone: 804-692-1298
Fax: 804-692-2209

Washington

Department of Social and Health
  Services
Division of Child Care and Early
  Learning
P.O. Box 45480
Olympia, WA 98504-5480
Phone: 360-413-3209
Fax: 360-413-3482

West Virginia

West Virginia Dept. of Health and
  Human Resources
Bureau for Children & Families
Office of Social Services, Div. of
  Planning Services
Child Care Services
350 Capitol Street, Room 691
Charleston,, WV 25301-3700
Phone: 304-558-2993
Fax: 304-558-8800

Wisconsin

Wisconsin Department of Workforce
  Development
Office of Child Care
201 East Washington Avenue, Room
  171
P.O. Box 7935
Madison, WI 53707-7935
Phone: 608-267-3708
Fax: 608-261-6968

Wyoming

Wyoming Department of Family
  Services
Hathaway Building Rm. 383
2300 Capitol Avenue
Cheyenne, WY 82002-0490
Phone: 307-777-6848
Fax: 307-777-3659

TOLL-FREE CHILD ABUSE REPORTING DIRECTORY

Each State designates specific agencies to receive and investigate reports of suspected child abuse and neglect. Typically, this responsibility is carried out by child protective services (CPS) within a Department of Social Services, Department of Human Resources, or Division of Family and Children Services. In some States, police departments also may receive reports of child abuse or neglect.

If, at any time, you are unsure of where to report child abuse or suspected child abuse, you will never go wrong if you contact your local police department for further assistance and further steps to take.

Many States have an in-State toll-free number, listed below, for reporting suspected abuse. The reporting party must be calling from the same State where the child is allegedly being abused for the following numbers to be valid.

For States not listed, or when the reporting party resides in a different State than the child, please call Childhelp, 800-4-A-Child (800-422-4453), or your local CPS agency.

Alaska (AK)
800-478-4444

Arizona (AZ)
888-SOS-CHILD (888-767-2445)

Arkansas (AR)
800-482-5964

Connecticut (CT)
800-842-2288
800-624-5518 (TDD/hearing impaired)

Delaware (DE)
800-292-9582

Florida (FL)
800-96-ABUSE (800-962-2873)

Illinois (IL)
800-252-2873

Indiana (IN)
800-800-5556

Iowa (IA)
800-362-2178

Kansas (KS)
800-922-5330

Kentucky (KY)
800-752-6200

Maine (ME)
800-452-1999

Maryland (MD)
800-332-6347

Massachusetts (MA)
800-792-5200

Michigan (MI)
800-942-4357

Mississippi (MS)
800-222-8000

Missouri (MO)
800-392-3738

Montana (MT)
800-332-6100

Nebraska (NE)
800-652-1999

Nevada (NV)
800-992-5757

New Hampshire (NH)
800-894-5533

New Jersey (NJ)
800-792-8610
800-835-5510 (TDD/hearing
impaired)

New Mexico (NM)
800-797-3260

New York (NY)
800-342-3720

North Carolina (NC)
Contact your County Department
of Social Services for the number of
Child Protective Services.

North Dakota (ND)
800-245-3736

Oklahoma (OK)
800-522-3511

Oregon (OR)
800-854-3508, ext. 2402

Pennsylvania (PA)
800-932-0313

Rhode Island (RI)
800-RI-CHILD (800-742-4453)

Texas (TX)
800-252-5400

Utah (UT)
800-678-9399

Virginia (VA)
800-552-7096

Washington (WA)
800-562-5624

West Virginia (WV)
800-352-6513

Wyoming (WY)
800-457-3659

ADDITIONAL RESOURCES

U.S. Department of Health and Human Services' Administration for Children and Families – After School Resources (General Services Administration)
[http://www.afterschool.gov]

One-stop access to government resources that support after school programs

Annie E. Casey Foundation
[http://www.aecf.org]

The Annie E. Casey Foundation (AECF) has worked to build better futures for disadvantaged children and their families in the United States. The primary mission of the Foundation is to foster public policies, human service reforms, and community supports that more effectively meet the needs of today's vulnerable children and families.

Child Care & Early Education Research Connections
[http://childcareresearch.org/discover/index.jsp]

Offering a comprehensive, up-to-date, and easy-to-use collection of more than 11,000 resources from the many disciplines related to child care and early education.

Child Care Aware
[http://www.childcareaware.org/en/]

Child Care Aware is a non-profit initiative committed to helping parents find the best information on locating quality child care and child care resources in their community.

Child Care Bureau
[http://www.acf.hhs.gov/programs/ccb/]

Child care and development
The Child Care and Development Fund
   Policies, research, and funding announcements

Child Care, Inc.
[http://www.childcareinc.org]
Child Care, Inc. offers a broad range of services to early childhood and school-age programs of all types. We offer affordable services to all programs, and provide special discounts.

Child Care Partnership Project
[http://nccic.org/ccpartnerships/home.htm]
How to create and maintain public and private partnerships for early childhood care and education programs

Child Outcomes Research & Evaluation, OPRE
[http://www.acf.hhs.gov/programs/opre/project/projectIndex.jsp#cc]
Publications, reports, and related documents on child care, Head Start, and early childhood education research efforts.

Child Welfare Information Gateway
[http://www.childwelfare.gov]
The Child Welfare Information Gateway provides access to information and resources to help protect children and strengthen families.

Early Childhood Outcomes Center, The
[http://www.fpg.unc.edu/~eco/index.cfm]
The ECO Center is a 5-year project funded by OSEP in October 2003. It is a collaborative effort of SRI International, FPG Child Development Institute at UNC-Chapel Hill, Juniper Gardens Children's Project, the National Association of State Directors of Special Education, and the University of Connecticut Health Center.

Healthy Child Care America
[http://nccic.org/hcca/]
The Healthy Child Care America campaign is a collaborative effort of health professionals, child care professionals, families and other services working in partnership to improve the health and well-being of children in child care settings.

National Association of Family Child Care
[http://www.nafcc.org]

The focus of NAFCC is to provide technical assistance to family child care associations. This assistance is provided through developing leadership and professionalism, addressing issues of diversity, and by promoting quality and professionalism through NAFCC's Family Child Care Accreditation.

National Child Care Information Center
[http://www.nccic.org]

National child care topics, issues, and research

Office of Special Education and Rehabilitative Services
[http://www.ed.gov/about/offices/list/osers/osep/index.html?src=mr]

The Office of Special Education Programs (OSEP) is dedicated to improving results for infants, toddlers, children and youth with disabilities ages birth through 21 by providing leadership and financial support to assist states and local districts.

Tribal Child Care Technical Assistance Center
[http://nccic.org/tribal/]

Materials for Tribal Child Care and Development Fund programs

USA Child Care
[http://www.usachildcare.org]

Supports local and state direct service provider associations committed to serving low- and moderate-income children.

Zero to Three ®
[http://www.zerotothree.org/site/PageServer?pagename=homepage]

ZERO TO THREE's mission is to support the healthy development and well-being of infants, toddlers and their families.

We are a national non-profit multidisciplinary organization that advances our mission by informing, educating and supporting adults who influence the lives of infants and toddlers.

GLOSSARY OF TERMS

Accredited — Accreditation is a seal of approval that may be applied to child care programs. It usually means the program has applied for the approval and meets some agreed upon standards of quality. Both the National Association for the Education of Young Children (NAEYC) and the National Accreditation Commission for Early Care and Education Programs (NAC) offer a center accreditation program.

Alternative Payment (AP) Program — A program of child care subsidy vouchers for low-income families administered through the California Department of Education and the Department of Social Services.

Background checks — The process of checking for history of criminal charges of potential child care providers before they are allowed to care for children.

Before and After-School Care — Programs where school-age children can be in supervised care before school begins and after school is out until the end of the work day.

Capacity — The total number of children that may be in care at any one time in a particular program.

Cardiopulmonary resuscitation (CPR) — Emergency measures performed by a person on another person whose breathing or heart activity has stopped. Measures include closed chest cardiac compressions and mouth-to-mouth ventilation in a regular sequence.

Center — Child care centers care for more than 12 children in a setting designed for learning program use. Children are usually separated by age groups and have group size limitations.

Certification Specialist — An employee of the Child Care Division responsible for assisting child care centers and group homes to comply with state licensing standards.

Certified Child Care Center — A business caring for more than 13 children in a facility designed for that purpose. Centers employ staff and are subject to staff-child ratios and annual announced and unannounced inspections.

Certified Child Care Group Home — A business caring for up to 12 children usually in the provider's home and subject to licensing requirements similar to Centers.

Child Care — The care, supervision and guidance on a regular basis of a child, unaccompanied by a parent, guardian or custodian, during a part of the 24 hours of the day, with or without compensation.

Child Care Center — A facility that is licensed to provide care of infants, toddlers, preschoolers, and/or school-age children all or part of the day. Centers may be large or small and can be operated independently or by a church or other organization. Most centers are licensed by the state Department of Social Services (DSS).

Child Care Management Agency (CMA) — In Alabama, there are 12 regional CMA's that serve as resource and referral agencies and that are responsible for the management of subsidized care.

Child Care Resource and Referral (CCR&R) Agency — A community-based organization that provides child care information and referrals to parents, training and assistance to providers, and outreach and education to businesses.

Child Care Worker — Defined by the Bureau of Labor Statistics as someone who attends to children at child care centers, schools, businesses, or institutions and performs a variety of tasks such as dressing, feeding, bathing, and overseeing play. (See **Preschool Teacher.**)

Child Development Associate Credential — A degree that requires at least 120 hours of formal preparation distributed across 6 goals and 13 functional areas of CDA competencies, at least 450 clock hours of experience working directly with children under supervision, and an independent assessment of the individual's competence for working with children.

Child Protective Services (CPS) — A program administered by the Department of Social Services to help children at risk of abuse or neglect within their families.

Commission for Child Care — 15 member commission appointed by the Governor, Speaker of the House and President of the Senate to address issues, problems, and solutions critical to the development of a balanced child care system.

Corporate Day Care Centers — Corporations may either fund or subsidize child care for their employee's children. Parents employed by these corporations are able to enroll their children in local day care centers in which the corporation has purchased spaces or in an on-site center. These centers must meet state licensing requirements.

Criminal History Check — A background check conducted by CCD, through the Law Enforcement Data System and state child protective services records on all child care providers, staff, and family members that may have unsupervised contact with children in care. The check may also include FBI records if the applicant is new to Oregon or is shown as a multi-state offender.

Criminal Records Background Check — A search of local, state, and/ or federal records to determine if a person has been convicted of a crime. Effective January 1, 1996, anyone working, or wanting to work, in child care must complete a criminal records background check. The results of the background check are used to decide if the person is fit to care for children.

Day Care Centers — In Alabama, a day care center is defined as a non-residential facility in which more than twelve children receive care during all or part of the day. In this type of care, children are grouped by age and developmental stage. Because day care centers provide care for large numbers of children, their hours of operation may be less flexible than other arrangements. All centers, with the exception of religious and school-based programs, must meet state licensing requirements for health and safety, staff-to-child ratios, caregiver qualifications, and curriculum. The parents of preschoolers are most likely to enroll their children in day care centers.

Developmentally Appropriate Practice — Child care that includes materials, activities, and staff expectations of children's behavior that are appropriate for a child's stage of development and that support the child's development and learning.

Director/Administrator — The person responsible for the on-site, ongoing daily supervision of the child care program and staff.

Early Childhood — Birth to age 8.

Exempt programs — Certain child care programs operated by churches and religious non-profit elementary schools which are exempt from the Department of Human Resource's licensing requirements.

Exempt Provider — A person or organization exempt from regulation in ORS 657A.250. These include providers caring for three or fewer children or children from only one family; programs operated by school districts; care provided in the home of the child or by a relative of the child; and limited duration programs such as summer youth camps.

Facility — The legal definition … The buildings, the grounds, the equipment, and the people involved in providing child care of any type.

Family Child Care Specialist — An employee of the Child Care Division responsible for assisting family child care providers to comply with state licensing standards.

Family Day Care Home — In Alabama, a "day care home," or family home, is a residential facility in which no more than six children receive care during the day. Like day care centers, family homes must meet state licensing requirements. Children in family home care are usually mixed in age. The small group size and home-based setting of family home care appeal particularly to parents of infants and toddlers.

Full Time Child Care — Care provided to children not yet eligible for the first grade or above. One or more children may fill a full-time space in the home as long as the children are not in care at the same time.

Group — Children who are assigned to a certain teaching staff member or team of staff members and who occupy an individual classroom or a well-defined physical space in a larger room.

Group Day Care Home — A group home is a residential facility in which at least seven and no more than ten children receive care. Group homes have two caregivers, a provider, and an assistant. This type of arrangement offers the same benefits as family home care.

Incremental Accreditation — A process that distinguishes between different levels of child care, from basic (care that meets minimum standards) through higher levels (care that strongly supports the development of children and that incorporates other services for families and children with special needs).

Infant — A child from birth to 12 months of age.

In-Home Care — Full-time or part-time child care arrangement where a friend, relative, or nanny cares for a child in the child's home.

License — A document issued by the State Department of Human Resources to a person, a group of people, or corporation who has met the state minimum standards for child care, which allows them to legally operate a child care program.

Minimum Standards — The minimum requirements of states to protect the health and safety of children in day care.

Mixed-Age Grouping — Placing children who are at least one year apart in age into the same child care group.

Non-Traditional Hours — Work hours other than 7 a.m. to 6 p.m., including evening, overnight, or weekend shifts. Child care needed during these hours is sometimes referred to as "odd hour" care.

Occasional Child Care — Care provided infrequently or intermittently, including but not limited to care that is provided during summer or other holiday breaks when children are not attending school.

Preschool or Nursery School — Programs that provide care for children who are three to five years old. They normally operate for three to four hours a day, and from two to five days a week.

Preschooler — A child between the ages of three and five.

Preschool Teacher — Defined by the Bureau of Labor Statistics as someone who instructs children (up to five years old) in activities designed to promote social, physical, and intellectual growth needed for primary school, in a preschool, child care center, or other child development facilities. A preschool teacher may be required to have a state certificate.

Process or Dynamic Quality — Interactions between children and their caregivers in a child care environment. This type of quality cannot be regulated because it is difficult to measure.

Professional Memberships — Early care providers are offered memberships in several local, state and national organizations geared toward enhancing the quality of child care in our community.

Registered Family Child Care Provider — A resident of a registered family child care home who is responsible for the children in care, is the children's primary caregiver, and whose name is on the certificate of registration.

Relative Care — Care provided by grandparents, siblings, and other family members. It is often the most affordable and convenient child care arrangement available to parents. Because of its flexibility, relative care is particularly popular among parents who work part-time or night shifts.

Resource and Referral Agency — Local organizations who give parents information about local day care centers or family day care homes. They also may provide training for child care providers, or work with the community to increase public awareness of the need for child care services.

Staff-to-Child Ratio — A ratio that represents the number of children per qualified caregiver in a child care program. For instance, Alabama requires at least one qualified caregiver for every six infants, or a 1:6 staff-to-child ratio.

Structural Quality — Characteristics including staff-to-child ratio, group size, staff education and experience, and square feet of facility per child. These characteristics can be regulated.

Subsidized Care — Financial assistance from state or federal funds available to low-income families who meet the state's income eligibility requirements. This type of care is available in licensed child care centers, in family child care homes, and by license-exempt providers.

Subsidy — Anything that either reduces the cost of providing care for children or that allows parents who normally could not afford care to enroll their children in a particular day care center.

Toddler — A child from 13 to 36 months of age.

PHOTO CREDITS

— TESTIMONIALS —

I wish I could have known of this resource recently when a single father was telling me about the problems he was having finding decent daycare for his son.

This book is perfect for men. Men need lists, and the checklists included are worth the price of the book alone.

Great job! Every new parent should have a copy.

ROBERT HILL — ALEXANDRIA, VA
WWW.SECRETSOFNETWORKMARKETERS.COM

"A Parent's Guide To Locating Responsible Child Care" is a wonderful resource.

Raising a child in today's world involves so many choices that a parent must be aware of in order to protect the health and welfare of their precious child.

"A Parent's Guide" explains your child care choices, provides resources and also includes convenient checklists to help you in your decision making.

It gives parents the questions to ask so they can get the best information regarding their child's care.

I highly recommend "A Parent's Guide To Locating Responsible Child Care" to all parents who will be placing their children in the hands of a care provider.

LORI STEFFEN — BALTIMORE, MD

There is no greater need in our society than protecting our children. They are our future and worth everything to protect. Every parent or would-be parent should consider this book a must read.

WARREN WHITLOCK — LAS VEGAS, NV — WWW.DAILYWARREN.COM

— TESTIMONIALS —

This is the indispensible resource that should always be available to every parent and grandparent. It serves as a guide and safety net in an age our children deserve (and need) every precaution provided here.

ELSOM ELDRIDGE, JR.; ED.M. (HARVARD) — WINTER SPRINGS, FL
CREATOR OF EXPLORING THE ARTS PROGRAM FOR AGES 3-5
WWW.OBVIOUS-EXPERT.COM

Every parent needs this Guide Book! It's probably THE MOST extensive book I've seen that can help you locate the kind of child care we all need. With all of the information in it, Ron has created an easy to follow format that is a breeze to use. In my line of work, I am particularly impressed with the underlying theme of locating or creating a positive atmosphere along with a safe environment and responsible care. It is NEVER too early to keep your child safe!

I wish I'd had this book when my boys were small!

JOYCE JACKSON — WALNUT CREEK, CA
CO-FOUNDER OF KEEPING KIDS SAFE ... KEEPING KIDS SAFE IS MY BUSINESS
WWW.KEEPINGKIDSSAFETODAY.COM

This is a beautiful book! Not only in the way you've produced it, but in the good that it will accomplish. When I look at parenting books, I get so tired of seeing the psycho-babble that passes for great parenting advice. New parents need a manual with clear, concise instructions. You've filled that gap with "A Parent's Guide to Locating Responsible Child Care: Discover How to Create A Safer Environment for Your Child." Filled with checklists, questionnaires and step-by-step instructions, any new parent, grandparent or child care provider will discover that this book is the ONLY book they'll need to ensure their child's safety as well as how to find the best child care providers.

And as a parent who raised three children, I wish I had read your instructions about creating a positive atmosphere for our kids ... it was perfect!

I now have four grandchildren ... I'm buying two copies of this book for their parents immediately!

DAVID PERDEW — EVA, AL
BAD DAD: 10 KEYS TO REGAINING TRUST
WWW.BAD-DAD.COM

— TESTIMONIALS —

Your "Parent's Guide to Locating Responsible Child Care" really hits the bull's-eye for a lot of parents who want to do the right thing and are scared to death of making a bad choice. Leaving our kids with someone other than a family member can be a nerve-wracking experience — especially if you don't know what to look for in a child care provider. Your book cuts through the scary situations and takes the guesswork out of finding a qualified caretaker for our kids. I love the tons of checklists and tips for finding the right person for each situation because they are quick and easy to follow.

The book also points out many things we wouldn't necessarily think about checking on when looking into a daycare center — from asking about educational programs and discipline strategies to proper hygiene and safety standards. It looks like you didn't leave anything out and I can sure recommend this as a "must-have-reference" for every parent.

KIM WEBB — SAN ANTONIO, TX
WWW.KNOWMORE.COM ... "SERVING PARENTS OF YOUNG CHILDREN"

My very first impression of Ron Capps' new book "A Parent's Guide to Locating Responsible Child Care: Discover How to Create a Safer Environment for Your Child," is in the title. He realizes that he is working with children and uses the term "child care."

I have had an ongoing battle with child care givers for twenty-five plus years over the term "child care" versus "day care." The thing is, we are working with children, not days, and that we are taking care of children, not days.

In one of my pastorates we had a child care center with approximately 100 children per day present. Fifty pre-schoolers with an educational program in place for them and fifty after-schoolers.

I realize the importance of a quality and safe environment for children.

From the title to the end, the book gives good advice for the parent looking for a quality, safe environment for their child.

I highly recommend this book.

"THE REAL SANTA" — JIM POLLARD — THE NORTH POLE
(SUMMER HOME — HICKORY, KY)
WWW.SANTASPEAKS.COM

— ACKNOWLEDGMENTS —

As I went through the process of creating this book, I was blessed by the encouragement of my wife Cindy and the thoughts of the joys and challenges that await my sons with the care and nurturing of their children.

I am a "Baby Boomer" and, as such, my family was exposed to the many new challenges of a changing workplace and community. My father was in the Armed Services. My mother was a working Registered Nurse. I faced health challenges and spent the first years of life being cared for by my grandparents.

Photos of my family look down upon me as I conclude this book. I am reminded of the blessings that I gained from being raised by a "non-traditional" parenting unit in the form of my grandparents. Nan and Dad were grounded in the traditions of a Texas family that still believed in traditional values and Sunday family gatherings. There were summers in the early 1950's where my grandfather found the time and energy to take me to virtually every Fresno Cardinal home game during the baseball season. This was after working 10 and 12 hours a day under the hot California sun. My grandparents always found time for me and encouraged me at every opportunity.

In some ways, my parents were among the first to face the challenges presented by today's society. I have recently wondered how different my life and that of my sister Susan might have been if they were to have had a guide like this to follow. For that matter, I wonder how different my relationship with my oldest son and his family might have been if I had known what I know now when I was raising him as a single parent.

I thank all of those named and unnamed who have contributed suggestions, encouragement and their skills to the creation of "A Parent's Guide to Locating Responsible Child Care."

— *Ronald R. Capps, Ph.D.*

— ABOUT THE AUTHOR —
Ronald R. Capps, Ph.D.

Ron and his wife Cindy live on 70 acres in northwest Missouri with an assortment of pets and native wildlife. In addition to being a parent and grandparent, Ron is a recognized international authority in Social Media and Communication and presently serves as an Adjunct Faculty Member to Missouri Western State University's Department of Communication in Saint Joseph, Missouri.

Ron holds assorted degrees from Louisiana State University, Pittsburg State University and California State University at Fresno. He has received numerous awards for his research skills and he has published and presented numerous reports and scholarly papers at national and professional conferences.

As the first release published as part of a series of releases from the Safeguard Children Organization, "A Parent's Guide to Locating Responsible Child Care: Discover How to Create A Safer Environment for Your Child" is dedicated to his grandchildren — Zoë, Mckenzie and Johnny and to all of the parents, grandparents and others who are interested in creating a safer environment for the children of the world.

CPSIA information can be obtained at www.ICGtesting.com
Printed in the USA
238429LV00006B/83/A